DUE D

Our Endangered Planet
TROPICAL RAIN FORESTS

Cornelia F. Mutel
and
Mary M. Rodgers

LERNER PUBLICATIONS COMPANY • MINNEAPOLIS

Thanks to Sharyn Fenwick, James E. Laib, Kerstin Coyle, Zachary Marell, and Gary Hansen for their help in preparing this book.

Words that appear in **bold** type are listed in a glossary that starts on page 60.

LIBRARY OF CONGRESS CATALOGING-IN-PUBLICATION DATA

Mutel, Cornelia Fleischer.
  Our endangered planet. Tropical rain forests / Cornelia F. Mutel and Mary M. Rodgers.
    p.   cm.
  Includes bibliographical references and index.
  Summary: Studies the ecology of tropical rain forests, or jungles, and the vital role of their water, air, plant, and animal resources in preserving the global environmental balance. Also describes how easily man's activities can endanger or upset this fragile environment.
  ISBN 0-8225-2503-8 (lib. bdg.)
  1. Rain forest ecology—Juvenile literature. 2. Rain forests—Juvenile literature. 3. Forest conservation—Tropics—Juvenile literature. 4. Deforestation—Tropics—Juvenile literature. [1. Rain forests. 2. Rain forest ecology. 3. Ecology.] I. Rodgers, Mary M. (Mary Madeline), 1954- . II. Title. III. Series: Our endangered planet (Minneapolis, Minn.)
QH541.5.R27M87 1991
333.75'0913—dc20   90-44354
                                              CIP
                                              AC
Manufactured in the United States of America

1 2 3 4 5 6 7 8 9 10 00 99 98 97 96 95 94 93 92 91

Front cover: Flames sweep through a tropical rain forest in Brazil, South America. Back cover: (Left) A worker jots down notes about a load of tropical timber cut from a forest in southeastern Mexico. (Right) This red-eyed tree frog clings to a branch of greenery in a Central American rain forest.

Recycled paper

All paper used in this book is of recycled material and may be recycled.

Recyclable

CONTENTS

OUR ENDANGERED PLANET

In the 1960s, astronauts first traveled beyond earth's protective atmosphere and were able to look back at our planet. What they saw was a beautiful globe, spinning slowly in space. That image reminds us that our home planet has limits, for no other place that we know of can support life.

The various parts of our natural environment—including air, water, plants, and animals—are partners in making our planet a good place to live. If we endanger one element, the other partners are badly affected, too.

People throughout the world are working to protect and heal earth's environment. They recognize that making nature our ally and not our victim is the way to shape a common future. Because we have only this one planet to share, its health and survival mean that we all can live.

Tropical rain forests cover only a small part of the earth, but they perform many complex jobs that affect the rest of the planet. For example, rain forests recycle water that falls as rain. They are home to countless kinds of animals and plants.

In the twentieth century, people have cut down many rain forests to create farmland. We are just beginning to understand the effects of this large-scale clearing. Certain types of plants and animals are wiped out as their homes disappear. Some scientists think that a rise in global temperatures may partly be caused by the loss of rain forests.

Rain forests cannot easily be replaced. We cannot replant them, and they take a long time to grow back naturally. By understanding the ways that rain forests support our planet's well-being, we can become strong activists in saving them.

CHAPTER ONE

IT'S A JUNGLE OUT THERE!

Halfway between the North and South Poles, hot, wet regions encircle the earth like a wide belt. Geographers call this belt the **tropics.** Here, rainfall is very high, the heat is constant, and **tropical rain forests** dominate the landscape.

Although they cover only about 6 percent of the earth's land surface, tropical rain forests contain more than half of the earth's **species,** or kinds, of living things. A few acres of rain forest in the Amazon River Basin, which stretches across much of central South America, hold more species of plants than all of Europe.

(Left) In most parts of a rain forest, very little sunlight reaches the floor. A person looking upward from the ground would see only the canopy, a dense, green covering that lets in narrow shafts of light.

Because of factors such as the warm, moist climate, rain-forest plants grow very fast. The leaves of some species are huge—sometimes big enough to shelter an adult human being.

INSIDE A RAIN FOREST

The great variety of life may not be obvious to a person walking through a tropical rain forest. The forest's floor is dark, quiet, and uncluttered. Rain-forest activity takes place high above the floor, in the **canopy**—the arched cover formed by the tops of trees. This living ceiling is home to two-thirds of the rain forest's plants and animals. Here, monkeys play, birds chatter, and flowers spring to life.

The canopy is so thick that it blocks sunlight from the lower rain forest. As a result,

7

rain-forest plants have developed many ways to reach the sunlight that they need to survive. Trees commonly grow to be 100 feet (31 meters) tall, and some giant species may reach 160 feet (49 meters) in height. These tall trees branch out only near the top, instead of lower down where their leaves would not get sunlight.

Lianas (climbing vines) wrap around tree trunks, reaching high before sprouting

A liana (left) sends out strong, finger-like shoots to attach itself to a rain-forest tree in southeastern Asia. Loose-hanging epiphytes (above) do not put their roots in soil. Instead, they anchor themselves to a host tree without harming it.

The spotted red petals of the rafflesia flower can grow to be one inch (2.5 centimeters) thick. A mature flower weighs as much as 15 pounds (6.8 kilograms). The plants are native to Indonesia in southeastern Asia.

shoots and leaves that tie the tops of trees into a dense mat of greenery. Smaller plants, called **epiphytes,** hang on the topmost branches of trees, getting food from dust, dripping water, and the remains of other animals and plants lying nearby.

Rain forests contain more animals than any zoo. Insects and birds are everywhere. The lush forests are home to many **primates** (a group of mammals that includes humans, apes, and lemurs). Some animals hide themselves by looking like another rain-forest object. For example, a katydid (a grasshopper) may be colored like the bark of a tree. Other rain-forest creatures are bright and showy or unusually large. The rafflesia flower, for instance, can grow to three feet (about one meter) in width.

Rain-forest animals and plants work together in very specific and complex ways.

Some acacia trees, for instance, provide homes and food for ants, which in turn sting other insects that might eat the acacias' leaves. Because certain plants and animals often depend on one another for survival, the loss of one species may mean the disappearance of several others.

Despite the wide variety of plants, nearly all rain forests have very old, very poor soils that cannot support long-term crop farming. The minerals in the soil, called **nutrients,** are also stored in the plants themselves and help rain forests to thrive. Plants and animals that die decay very rapidly. As they rot, they release nutrients back into the soil. The nutrients feed other living things.

THE EARTH'S GREEN BELT

Not all tropical forests are the same. **Lowland evergreen forests** flourish in places where the climate never changes. Without a cool or dry period to slow plant growth, these rain forests are always green, wet, growing, and active. Lowland evergreen

forests are the biggest, most varied, and lushest of all tropical forests. They hold the largest number of different species.

Cloud forests, which are cooler than the lowland forests, cling to the sides of

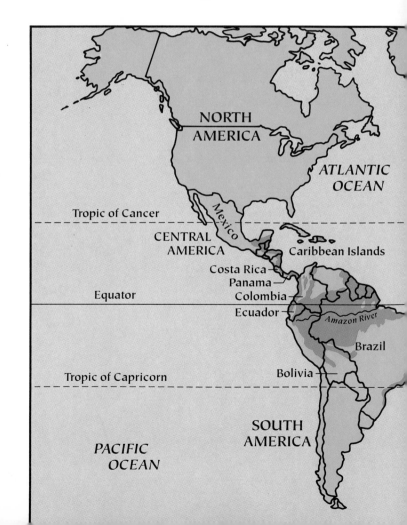

mountains. Cloudlike mist drifts through these extremely moist rain forests all day long. Mosses, ferns, and epiphytes color the constantly dripping trees a bright green.

Seasonal rain forests grow in tropical areas where dry weather regularly interrupts the warm, wet climate. This change slows plant growth and forest activity. Seasonal rain forests do not support

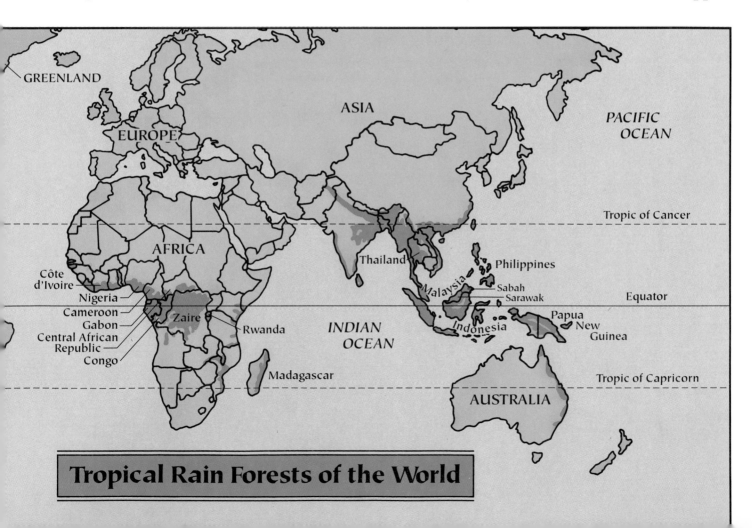

Tropical Rain Forests of the World

An aerial view of Indonesia's lowland rain forests (left) shows an almost unbroken canopy. Sunlight (below) reaches the ground-dwelling plants of this jungle in Costa Rica, a small nation in Central America.

as many different species as evergreen forests do.

Wherever sunlight reaches the forest floor, younger, smaller trees and plants thrive. They form a dense, tangled mass of growth, sometimes called a **jungle.** Jungles are found at the edges of rain forests, along rivers, and in patches within the forest where trees have fallen. Jungles also grow where forests have been cut.

A logger poses between piles of tropical timber cut from a Central American rain forest.

Bananas, guavas, oranges, papayas, and mangoes are popular tropical fruits.

TROPICAL TRIVIA

 Tropical rain forests receive at least 80 inches (203 centimeters) and as much as 320 inches (813 centimeters) of rainfall each year.

The loss of rain forests causes several species of plants and animals to become extinct *every day.*

Many medicines used in the United States originally came from rain-forest plants or animals.

The tarsier, which lives in Asia's rain forests, is the smallest monkey in the world.

Tropical rain forests hold more kinds of plants and animals than any other natural community.

Japan, the United States, and Western Europe import most of the world's tropical hardwoods. Japan's wood imports come from Southeast Asia. The United States gets its imports mostly from Brazil, and Europe's are shipped from West Africa.

Foods and spices that originated in tropical rain forests include bananas, oranges, paprika, black pepper, cinnamon, and tomatoes.

In Rwanda, central Africa, a female mountain gorilla named Liz relaxes in the tropical sunshine. Gorillas live exclusively in the rain forests of Africa, where their only enemies are humans who hunt them, capture them, or destroy their living space.

In time, if left alone, these jungles could become new rain forests.

A UNIQUE STOREHOUSE

Although rain forests around the world might all look the same, they contain different types of animals and plants. More than any other living communities, rain forests have a large percentage of **endemic species**—plants or animals that are found only in one area.

For example, Brazil nut trees grow only in the Amazon River Basin. Gorillas are limited to central Africa. Giant trees called **dipterocarps** dominate the rain forests in Southeast Asia. Most of the primates and flowering plants on Madagascar (an island off the eastern coast of Africa) exist nowhere else on earth.

Because they live in specific areas, endemic species can easily become **extinct,** that is, die out completely. If we destroy the only place on our planet where these species live, they will disappear forever.

Various rain-forest peoples are also threatened by the destruction of the forests. These groups rely on tropical plants and animals for food, fuel, building materials, and medicines. These peoples have found ways to live in rain forests without damaging them. Over the centuries, they have become part of the rain forest's natural community.

For centuries, the world's rain forests have sheltered peoples who are part of the forests' natural community. In central Africa dwell the Aka (left), whom scientists believe were the earliest group to live in the continent's rain forests. An Iban man (right) prepares his son for a local ceremony in Malaysia's forests.

CHAPTER TWO

EARTH'S TREASURE-HOUSE

Every day, people throughout the world benefit from the products of tropical rain forests. Cacao (the source of chocolate), bananas, cinnamon, cloves, and sugarcane are a few of the many foods that originated in tropical forests. These forests also provided the first peanuts, rice, yams, and coffee beans. The raw materials of many common products come from tropical forests and turn up in things we use daily, such as furniture, cough drops, golf balls, perfume, and jogging shoes.

In addition to food and raw materials, rain-forest plants provide many important

(Left) A bromeliad—an epiphyte whose upturned leaves capture water—provides moisture and a breeding ground to animals that live in the canopy. (Right) Workers in Costa Rica sort through red cacao beans that come from the country's tropical rain forests.

medicines. Some of our drugs for treating leukemia, high blood pressure, and malaria originated in rain forests. Scientists think that tropical plants may even hold the secret to curing some forms of cancer. Rainforest dwellers also use the plants to treat illnesses ranging from arthritis and fever to skin infections and snakebite.

The source of these foods, raw materials, and medicines is the rain forest's spectacular variety of plants and animals. Biologists estimate that the earth contains

Scarlet tanagers nest in North America and fly to Central and South America in the fall. In the warm climate of the tropics, the birds cast off their feathers and feed on local insects and berries.

from 5 to 30 million different species, over half of which live in the tropics. This rainforest feature—its many different kinds of living things—is known as **biodiversity.** Within a given area, however, may dwell only a few members of each separate species.

Scientists have identified less than 2 million of the earth's species. Experts have examined a much smaller number for useful products or chemicals. The millions of unidentified, unexamined tropical species may provide medical cures, sources of fuel, natural **pesticides** (pest killers), and food sources.

A GLOBAL ROLE

Rain forests also support species that live elsewhere on our planet. For example, scientists have traced major declines of North American songbirds—such as warblers, vireos, and tanagers—to the loss of tropical forests. Almost half of these bird species spend the winter in the tropical lands of Central America and the Caribbean Islands.

LIFE-SAVING PLANTS

Greg Marsh is 12, and for the past five years he has had **lymphocytic leukemia.** This blood disease is a form of cancer that usually affects children. In Greg's case, the lymphocytes—his body's white blood cells—are multiplying very fast. Because Greg has too many white cells, his system has trouble making red blood cells. The red cells are needed to carry oxygen to all parts of the human body.

After doctors pinpointed Greg's disease, he began to take an anti-leukemia drug made from the rosy periwinkle. This pink flower once grew only in the rain forests of the island of Madagascar. About 15 tons [13.6 metric tons] of periwinkle leaves are needed to make 1 ounce [28 grams] of the drug.

The odd thing is, chemists examined the periwinkle for medicinal properties and did not find any. Later, local healers on Madagascar shared their knowledge of the plant with researchers. They re-examined the flower and discovered its value as an anti-cancer agent.

The leaves, not the petals, of the rosy periwinkle contain a valuable anti-cancer medicine.

Since the mid-1980s, thanks to the periwinkle, a person with lymphocytic leukemia has had a 99-percent chance that the disease will go into remission. This means that the symptoms will disappear, at least for a while. If Greg's condition had not been treated, he might have died.

Rain-forest losses could have wiped out all of the world's periwinkles before scientists learned of their value. As we cut down more forests, we lose other plants whose benefits are not yet known to us. In many cases, researchers need the help of traditional healers to figure out which plants are worth investigating.

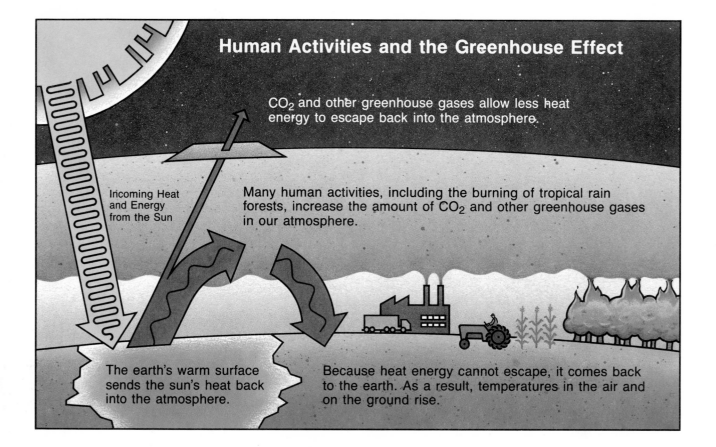

Human Activities and the Greenhouse Effect

CO_2 and other greenhouse gases allow less heat energy to escape back into the atmosphere.

Incoming Heat and Energy from the Sun

Many human activities, including the burning of tropical rain forests, increase the amount of CO_2 and other greenhouse gases in our atmosphere.

The earth's warm surface sends the sun's heat back into the atmosphere.

Because heat energy cannot escape, it comes back to the earth. As a result, temperatures in the air and on the ground rise.

As tropical rain forests shrink in these areas, fewer songbirds survive the winter. Thus fewer birds return to breed in southern Canada and in the northern and central United States in the summer.

Rain forests also play a major role in the earth's climate. Much of the living material in rain forests is made of carbon. When people burn rain forests to clear the land, they release carbon into the air as a gas

The millions of green plants in tropical rain forests absorb poisonous carbon dioxide (CO₂) during photosynthesis—a complex process that uses CO₂, sunlight, and water to make food.

called **carbon dioxide (CO$_2$).** In 1989, loss of tropical forests sent an estimated 2.4 billion tons (2.2 billion metric tons) of CO$_2$ into the atmosphere. This much gas would fill 510 million hot-air balloons!

As CO$_2$ rises into the atmosphere, it traps the earth's heat. Scientists fear that this process—sometimes called the **greenhouse effect**—may increase the earth's temperature over the next several decades. At higher temperatures, ice-covered areas of the earth could melt and sea levels could rise. Summers might be longer and hotter, and rainfall might decrease.

The green plants in tropical rain forests also absorb CO$_2$ as part of a complex food-making process called **photosynthesis.** As we cut down rain forests, we reduce the number of green plants that take in CO$_2$.

SOIL SAVERS

Rain forests also protect **topsoil** (the upper layer of dirt) and regulate the flow and quality of river water. For example, falling rain slowly drips off leaves and branches in the rain forest and soaks into the soil. Plant roots absorb more than half of the

In a healthy rain forest, rainfall that reaches the ground collects in small streams and narrow waterfalls (above) and eventually feeds large rivers. Some of the rainwater is taken up by the roots of plants, which return the moisture to the air through their leaves and petals (right).

rainfall. Plants then return this moisture to the atmosphere through their leaves as water vapor. The water vapor collects in storm clouds and falls to the earth again as rain. Thus the forest makes rain by continuously recycling water.

Water that is not absorbed by plants slowly trickles down to rivers. Healthy rain forests release water in steady, clean streams, rather than in muddy bursts that cause destructive floods.

When we cut down rain forests, we remove more than just trees and other plants. We also stop the forests from preventing environmental problems, from protecting natural communities, from absorbing CO_2, and from maintaining rainfall levels.

Cutting down trees and other rain-forest plants exposes the soil to the destructive force of water. These bare hills in Madagascar were once covered with rain forests. Rainfall easily carries topsoil from the hills to river valleys.

CHAPTER THREE

OUR VANISHING RAIN FORESTS

Most of the world's remaining rain forests are being rapidly cleared through cutting and burning—a process called **deforestation**—to make cropland and pasture. Almost half of the world's original four billion acres (1.6 billion hectares) of rain forests are now gone. The lost area equals the combined size of Washington, Idaho, California, Nevada, and Arizona. Most of the large-scale clearing has happened since the mid-1900s, when populations began to expand rapidly in the tropics and pressure for more farmland grew.

Experts disagree about the rate of rain-forest destruction. Estimates range from 50 to 125 acres (20 to 51 hectares) each minute. This means that every 60 seconds roughly 100 football fields of rain forest go up in smoke. In a year, these minute-by-minute losses add up to millions of acres. If current trends are not changed, rain forests may disappear in the twenty-first century.

FARMS ON FIRE

In general, a few rich landowners hold the best farmland in the tropics and hire people to work on their plantations. These large farms usually grow food or raise cattle for beef to sell to foreign countries. Little of what the plantations produce remains in tropical nations. This situation leaves only the land with poor soil for everyone else to use to grow food.

(Left) Fallen trees and charred vegetation litter the floor of a burning rain forest in Brazil's Amazon River Basin.

The populations of tropical countries are increasing at a fast rate. Growing numbers of people lack jobs and are unable to support their families. Many tropical governments have encouraged their poorest citizens to move into the rain forests.

These landless, unemployed people view the governments' plans as opportunities to make their lives better. After claiming a small piece of land, these new settlers clear it. Their method of clearing land, called **slash-and-burn farming,** is probably

In rain forests throughout the world, families use slash-and-burn methods to create new farmland. First, they cut down trees and other plants (above). Then, the farmers set fire to the vegetation (right).

the most common destroyer of the world's tropical forests.

A family practices slash-and-burn farming by cutting forests and then burning the remaining vegetation. The family members plant crops, which grow well in the first year. Each season, however, the soil's fertility decreases and harvests decline. Insects and weeds become problems. Within a few years, the poor tropical soils can no longer support the family. It moves away in search of another forest plot to clear.

After the charred field is level, the slash-and-burn farmers plow the soil (left) and plant crops (above). Food grows for a few seasons, but the soil lacks the nutrients it needs to be productive for a long time.

People have practiced slash-and-burn farming for centuries. In previous times, the amount of land used in this way was small, and abandoned farm plots could recover their fertility. But now, as many as 250 million slash-and-burn farmers cut down between 15 and 50 million acres (6 and 20 million hectares) of forest each year. This annual loss is equal in size to the state of Nebraska.

Some of these settlers are even illegally clearing parks and nature preserves, which are supposed to be protected against change. As a result of widespread slash-and-burn methods, large sections of rain forests have become too weak from overuse and lack of nutrients to grow back.

TREES AS BUSINESS

Large-scale timber cutting, called **logging,** is also a major cause of rain-forest destruction. Sometimes this wood is used as fuel in factories within a tropical country. More often, the wood is sold to other nations.

Japan imports half of all the tropical timber harvested each year, mostly from Southeast Asia. Japan's large logging companies are now attempting to expand their activities into the vast forests of the Amazon River Basin.

In the darkness of an African rain forest, a logger uses a chain saw to slice through the roots of a tree.

A worker inspects a truckload of tropical timber before the vehicle leaves a logging camp in southeastern Mexico. The area's stands of mahogany, rosewood, and ebony are cut down and sold abroad as raw material for furniture and other goods. The Mexican government is bringing settlers into the region to become slash-and-burn farmers. As a result of logging and farming, Mexico's last sections of rain forest are disappearing.

JAPAN SWINGS A HEAVY AX

Two-thirds of Japan is covered with woodlands, which the Japanese carefully tend. Each year, however, Japan imports half of all the tropical hardwood timber cut down in the world's rain forests. The Japanese value the strength and beauty of tropical wood. They use it to build their houses and furniture. The Japanese also make tropical hardwood into paper and cardboard boxes.

Most of Japan's sources of tropical wood lie in Southeast Asia, specifically in Malaysia, Indonesia, and the Philippine Islands. Large Japanese trading companies import most of the tropical timber, supplying factories with the logs to produce plywood, for example. This thin, sturdy wood is a popular building material for Japanese houses.

Because of public and private pressure, the Japanese government has begun to accept some responsibility for preserving tropical rain forests. Efforts are under way to educate Japanese consumers about substitutes for tropical hardwoods in making homes, furniture, and paper. Some groups are pushing for laws that would force Japanese trading companies to manage their logging operations wisely. These moves could help Southeast Asia's tropical rain forests to survive.

A store in Japan offers a wide variety of goods made from tropical wood.

The United States and Western Europe also import large amounts of tropical timber, such as teak, rosewood, and mahogany. Tropical woods are made into many items, including toilet paper, chopsticks, matches, furniture, cardboard boxes, and musical instruments.

Logging companies have concentrated on forests in Southeast Asia and West Africa. Some countries in those regions have already lost nearly all of their rain forests. Many more nations will have cleared their loggable forests by the year 2000.

In most cases, the methods used to cut timber are unwise. Loggers often clear entire forests and do not replant cut areas. Sometimes workers take just the largest or the most valuable trees. While harvesting trees, the loggers often damage the remaining forest. For example, as cut trees fall, they injure or pull down saplings (young trees) or surrounding mature trees.

Heavy logging machinery packs down the soil so that plant seedlings cannot grow. The topsoil is easily washed away

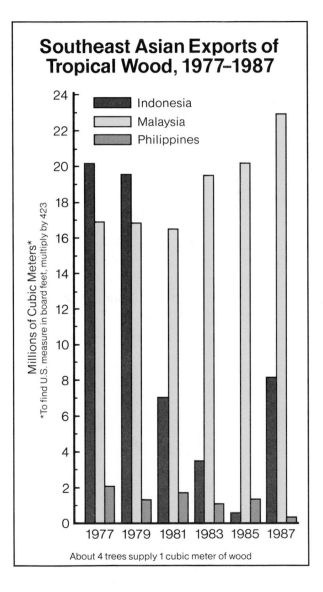

Southeast Asian Exports of Tropical Wood, 1977–1987

Millions of Cubic Meters*

*To find U.S. measure in board feet, multiply by 423

- Indonesia
- Malaysia
- Philippines

About 4 trees supply 1 cubic meter of wood

during rainstorms. In addition, tropical logging operations waste a large amount of usable wood by leaving it in the forest to rot.

Cows graze on a recently cleared piece of rain-forest land. Cattle ranchers have destroyed large areas of rain forest in South and Central America to create grassland for their livestock. In a short time, however, the pastures lose their productivity, and the ranchers abandon the old plots for new ones.

CATTLE RANCHING

The creation of vast cattle ranches is another big cause of rain-forest loss. Cattle ranching increased in Central America in the 1960s, when the United States started to import a large amount of beef from that region. Beef prices in the United States were high, and the fast-food industry needed a low-cost supply of hamburger meat.

In Brazil, landowners have made more than 25 million acres (10 million hectares) of rain forest into cattle ranches. This area equals the size of the state of Kentucky. Brazilian ranchers either buy land cleared by slash-and-burn farmers or clear the forests themselves. On many days, smoke from hundreds of rain-forest fires hovers over Brazil.

Often workers do not remove any trees before the burning begins. As a result, fires destroy valuable tropical timber. Once converted to pasture, ranchers may burn the land again and again to encourage grass to grow and to keep out poisonous weeds. As happens on small crop farms, the repeated

Meat packers prepare beef carcasses for shipment abroad. The rise in U.S. demand for cheap sources of beef sparked the expansion of cattle ranching in South and Central America.

fires decrease the land's productivity year after year.

Eventually, the ranchers abandon worn-out pastures and move on to claim new rain-forest land. In most cases, the abandoned pasture does not have the natural strength or nutrients to grow trees again. As a result, our planet loses its valuable rain forests forever.

"PROGRESS" CAN BE COSTLY

Farmers, loggers, and landowners are not the only groups that destroy rain forests. To help vehicles and people move within rain forests, tropical governments and foreign companies have blasted through the dense growth to lay roads. The roads allow work crews, supply trucks, and heavy equipment to enter the forests. The roads

Two young girls from Ecuador in South America play on an oil pipeline that cuts through their country's rain forests. Many industrial projects that are meant to improve local economies end up severely damaging tropical rain forests.

also bring slash-and-burn farmers into new areas of the rain forests.

Most projects intended to help poor countries severely damage rain forests. International banks, for example, have loaned money to tropical countries so that they can become more industrialized. With more industries, many people believe, these less-developed nations could make money and create jobs.

Among the many large-scale projects funded by such banks are **hydroelectric dams.** Built across rivers, these structures control the flow of water to make electricity. The electrical power provides energy to industries. This type of power is especially important in tropical countries, where other energy sources, such as coal and petroleum, are scarce.

Unfortunately, the dams also flood huge sections of the rain forest, destroying the natural homes of people, plants, and animals. Some new dams never control enough water to create electricity. Thus the benefits they offered do not last long but the destruction remains.

Other large projects in tropical countries produce lumber, wood-pulp chips, iron, and bauxite (the raw material for making aluminum). Most of these goods go to people in richer nations. People who live in rain-forest regions usually do not directly benefit from these businesses. Their governments, however, are still responsible for paying back the loans that started the projects.

GOING UP IN SMOKE

The results of destroying the rain forests are the same no matter how the forests are cleared. Global weather patterns change, rare plants and animals become extinct, and pollution increases. Loss of rain forests causes regional environmental problems—such as **erosion** (the washing away of topsoil), flooding, and damage to food sources.

Different types of projects harm rain forests in different ways. Hydroelectric dams, for example, create lakes where flies, mosquitoes, and snails can breed. These tiny pests can transmit serious illnesses to local people. Mining operations may release mercury, a highly poisonous metal, into rivers that flow through the rain forests.

When rain forests are cleared, the original residents lose their source of medicine, food, building material, and income. New settlers bring in diseases that kill many rain-forest peoples and damage age-old ways of life. In 1500, the Amazon River Basin held at least six million Indians. By 1900, the population had dropped to one million. Fewer than 200,000 now remain.

The clearing of forests destroys the **habitats,** or natural homes, of many animals and plants. Scientists estimate that at least 4,000 tropical species become extinct each year. The rate of extinction for rain forests is faster than it is for any other natural community on earth. Once these living things disappear, our planet loses the biodiversity and potential benefits they offered.

The golden marmoset or tamarin—a type of monkey—is native to the rain forests of Panama and South America. The species is now endangered because its habitat is shrinking.

CHAPTER FOUR

RAIN FORESTS AROUND THE WORLD

Rain forests are found in three major areas, namely Latin America, Southeast Asia, and Africa. Three countries—Brazil in Latin America, Indonesia in Southeast Asia, and Zaire in Africa—together contain about half of the world's remaining rain forests.

LATIN AMERICA

Latin America's rain forests originally covered portions of Central America, South America, and the Caribbean Islands. These regions now hold about three-fifths of the world's remaining rain forests. Workers have cleared most of the rain forests of Central America and the Caribbean Islands.

The largest expanse of rain forest remains in the Amazon River Basin, which is located in Brazil and in the countries that

(Left) Because rain-forest soils are so poor, tree roots often seek nourishment in the shallow topsoil rather than deep in the ground. Buttress roots flutter from a tree trunk, creating protective bays for other vegetation. (Above) The large, brilliantly colored beak of a toco toucan helps the bird to find a mate in Brazil's tropical rain forests.

border Brazil. Through this vast region flows the powerful Amazon River—the world's biggest river system.

Work crews have cut down large sections of Brazil's rain forest within the last few years. Only a tiny bit of the country's coastal rain forests remain. Brazil's inland Amazon rain forests are still very large. But slash-and-burn farming, industrial projects, logging, and ranching threaten the existence of these forests.

The Brazilian government sees its forests as a source of wealth and has encouraged some industrial projects that have destroyed large areas of rain forest. Nations around the world have criticized Brazil for sacrificing its rain forests for financial gain.

Even the international banks that loan Brazil money have felt public pressure to stop rain-forest destruction. They are starting to withhold loans worth hundreds of millions of dollars until the Brazilian government agrees to protect the forests and the peoples who live in them. Because of this pressure, Brazil's approach to rain-forest use seems to be changing.

CHICO MENDES
Defending a Way of Life

Chico Mendes grew up in the rain forests of northwestern Brazil in the 1950s. His father, a rubber tapper (collector), showed him how to make careful, slanting cuts in the bark of rubber trees. Through the cuts oozed a milky white sap, called **latex,** which drips into small cups tied to the trees. The tappers sell the latex to companies that use it to make rubber. A rebel soldier who was hiding in the forests taught young Chico to read and to think for himself. These lessons influenced Mendes as an adult when he became a strong voice in defense of Brazil's rubber tappers and of the Amazon rain forests that provide their livelihoods.

Chico Mendes (pictured here with his wife, Ilzamar) lived and worked in the rain forests of Brazil.

In the 1970s, Brazil's powerful cattle ranchers cut and burned thousands of acres of rain forest to create pasture. To protest this destruction, Mendes and other rubber tappers formed the Rural Workers Union. In peaceful ways, they resisted the loss of the forests. For example, when a rain-forest section was marked for clearing, rubber tappers and their families would gather at the site to talk the harvesters out of cutting down trees.

By the 1980s, Mendes was well known outside Brazil and often attended conferences in the United States and Europe. At these meetings, he urged banks and other groups that lend money to tropical countries to safeguard the forests. He showed the lenders that rain forests can provide valuable goods within protected zones called extractive reserves. Through careful management, these zones can supply food and raw materials for generations to come.

In the late 1980s, Mendes's work was paying off. The Brazilian government had established several extractive reserves. This success, however, angered powerful landowners. Violence against union members and

Slanting cuts in the bark of a rubber tree guide the sap into a small cup.

death threats against Mendes became common. In December 1988, at age 44, Mendes was killed outside his home in the Amazon rain forest. The sons of a local cattle rancher were charged with Mendes's murder.

Mendes devoted his life to defending the rain forests and the rights of rubber tappers. Although his murder saddened people around the world, his death also made them more aware of his goals and spurred efforts to save the rain forests.

Colombia, in northwestern South America, also has been affected by expanding cattle ranches, intensive logging programs, and slash-and-burn farming. Rain forests remain in Colombia's section of the Amazon River Basin and along the coast of the Pacific Ocean. Scientists believe that these areas contain more plant and animal species than any other rain forests in the world except Brazil's. Thousands of Indians also inhabit Colombia's rain forests.

Despite pressures to develop industries in its rain forests, the Colombian government has strongly supported conservation efforts. By 1990, it had granted full legal control of more than one-half of its Amazon rain forests to its rain-forest Indians.

The grant protected 69,000 square miles (178,700 square kilometers)—an area equal to the size of the state of Missouri. The government cannot log, mine, or sell this land. Colombian officials encourage the Indians to preserve their traditional lifestyle because it protects the forests.

SOUTHEAST ASIA

Rain forests originally covered much of Southeast Asia, including the Philippine Islands, Thailand, Malaysia, and Indonesia. Big forests now exist only on certain

Although some of Colombia's rain forests have been damaged, the government has given large tracts to the country's rain-forest peoples. They protect the forests from further harm by living in traditional ways that do not abuse the land.

large islands of Southeast Asia. The region's rain forests provide the world with most of its tropical hardwoods. Workers cut or damage more than 6 million acres (2.4 million hectares) of trees every year. This area equals the size of the state of New Hampshire.

A nation made up of thousands of islands, Indonesia has the world's largest rain forests after Brazil's. Indonesia's extremely varied forests contain 515 kinds of mammals—more than any other country—and 1,500 types of birds. Tigers, orangutans, birds of paradise, and tree wallabies are a few of the nation's unusual species.

Some areas of Indonesia's rain forests are being deforested very quickly. Logging companies do much of the damage as they harvest wood. But another source of deforestation is a government program that has moved millions of Indonesians from crowded islands to the sparsely populated rain forests. This movement is called **resettlement.**

To build farms and to establish villages, new settlers have cleared or seriously

A woman from Indonesia carefully arranges sticks of cinnamon to dry. The spice comes from the bark of cinnamon trees that grow in the nation's rain forests.

damaged more than 120 million acres (49 million hectares) of rain forest. This area is almost as big as the states of Utah and Colorado combined.

Indonesia's resettlement program started in the 1950s. It was supposed to solve lack

Indonesia's resettlement program brought thousands of new residents into the country's undisturbed rain forests. Although the government has slowed its resettlement plans, these people are still cutting down trees for use as fuel.

of housing and other problems for the country's rapidly growing population. In addition, the nation's leaders believed the program would keep the outer forested islands—places of political unrest—under governmental control. International banks and foreign countries paid for the Indonesian government's resettlement plans.

The program has caused severe environmental problems, including erosion and flooding. Year after year, the poor soils in rain forests grow less rice and other crops that the settlers need to live. Indonesia's leaders have slowed the program because of these problems and because they are running out of money.

Much of the world's tropical hardwood comes from the Malaysian states of Sarawak and Sabah. These states occupy the northern part of Borneo—a large island in the South China Sea. Japan is the region's biggest customer, importing 90 percent of its logs from Sarawak and Sabah.

Almost half of Sabah's income comes from its forestry activities, and the government claims that most of the state's forests are ready for harvesting. A new law makes it a crime to try to stop a logging company from cutting down timber. Loggers have probably cleared or injured 70 percent of Sabah's forest.

The forests in Sarawak, a state in Malaysia, contain many unusual animal species. The Raja Brooke butterfly is named after James Brooke, the British adventurer who once governed the region.

Tropical hardwood logs from Sarawak's shrinking forests await transportation on the Baram River.

In many cases, logging practices—such as making roads to move equipment and clearing nearby land to strip leaves off the logs—do more damage than the actual cutting of trees does. For every two trees felled in Sabah, harvesters usually destroy half an acre (one-tenth of a hectare) of healthy rain forest.

AFRICA

Africa's rain forests line the coast of West Africa and grow along the Zaire River, which flows through the west central part of the continent. Cameroon, Congo, Gabon, and Zaire have thick forests, and these nations harvest them for timber and minerals.

One-fourth of Africa's rain forests have disappeared since 1950. Slash-and-burn farming and commercial logging have caused the destruction. West African forests have been especially heavily used. Côte d'Ivoire (formerly Ivory Coast), for example, has lost nearly 90 percent of its forests in less than 30 years.

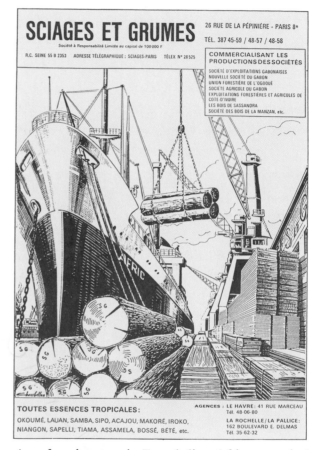

An advertisement in French lists African tropical timber available to the European market. Many of the companies listed as suppliers get their wood from Gabon, which lies on the West African coast. Gabon's forests, which are located in the Zaire River Basin, provide a large share of the nation's foreign income.

Rain forests also grow in eastern Madagascar, a thousand-mile-long island that lies 250 miles (402 kilometers) off Africa's eastern coast. The island contains a great number of endemic species. Over four-fifths of its primates, reptiles, mammals, and flowering plants are found nowhere else.

Eastern Madagascar was once nearly covered with rain forests. In 1990, about one-fifth of the original area remained forested. Slash-and-burn farmers are responsible for much of the damage. Poverty and a rapidly expanding population have sped up the farmers' land-clearing activities. As food becomes scarce and expensive, farmers cut down more rain forests to care for their growing families. Cattle ranching and logging are responsible for the rest of the destruction.

Massive tree cutting has deforested this hillside in eastern Madagascar.

CHAPTER FIVE

WORLDWIDE CONSERVATION EFFORTS

Many governments, groups, and individuals throughout the world have become aware of the far-reaching effects of rain-forest losses. They have come up with many plans to save at least some of the world's rain forests.

For example, conservationists (people who work to protect our environment) are asking international banks to stop loaning money for projects that destroy rain forests. Some banks, in turn, are forcing leaders of rain-forest countries to slow deforesta-tion. Some banks are looking for rain-forest conservation projects that they can fund.

In recent years, people living within tropical countries have become a major influence for change. Between 1970 and 1990, for example, people formed more than 300 conservation organizations in Brazil alone. In Malaysia, the nomadic Penan people may lose their ancient forests to logging companies. In response, the Penan have risked arrest by repeatedly blocking the logging roads.

Plans to preserve rain forests vary. Some of the many suggestions include placing rain forests in permanent preserves and increasing the non-destructive uses of the forests. Other proposals encourage scientific understanding of these forests through research and point out the need to fully fund conservation efforts.

(Left) As Madagascar's forests disappear, fewer of its unique species are able to find habitats. These sifaka lemurs cling to trees with their powerful hind legs and can fly from trunk to trunk with amazing ease. Many people are worried that lemurs, which live only on Madagascar, may soon become extinct as their fragile environment disappears.

SETTING LAND ASIDE

Governments and other organizations have set aside sections of rain forests as protected zones. Some of these areas are only for native animals and plants, and people are not allowed to settle in them. But many preserves allow the human residents already present to remain and to carry out non-destructive activities.

Some tropical governments have established **extractive reserves** in which resident families are allowed to extract (collect) rain-forest products, such as natural rubber and Brazil nuts. In the late 1980s, Brazil formed several of these reserves, which permanently safeguarded the rights of rubber tappers and other rain-forest dwellers. For a long time, these groups

This Waiwai Indian lives and works in an extractive reserve in Brazil. The reserve yields money-earning crops without damaging the forest's natural communities of animals and plants.

disagreed with cattle ranchers about how to use the forests.

Usually, tropical countries do not have the funds to pay rangers to police their rain-forest preserves. Conservation groups give money, training, and advice to help these nations protect their preserves from slash-and-burn farmers, hunters, fires, and other sources of damage.

USE WITHOUT ABUSE

Most rain-forest destruction occurs for economic reasons. Officials in tropical governments and some foreign companies see the forests as a quick way to make money. They do not always realize that logging, ranching, and other actions bring short-term profits and long-term losses.

Conservationists want tropical governments to try **sustainable development**—harvesting rain-forest products over a long period without injuring the forests. These activists point out that profits from rain-forest products often are greater than gains from logging or farming.

A boy holds an opened Brazil nut fruit that contains several tree seeds. After removing the hard shells, people eat the seeds as nuts. The seeds can also be ground into a valuable cooking oil.

For example, the income from wild rubber trees and Brazil nut trees in one part of Brazil is four times greater than earnings from cattle ranching in the same area. This fact and others persuaded the Brazilian government to establish the first extractive reserves. Many conservationists feel that carefully managed sustainable development is the key to the survival both of rain forests and of the people who live in them.

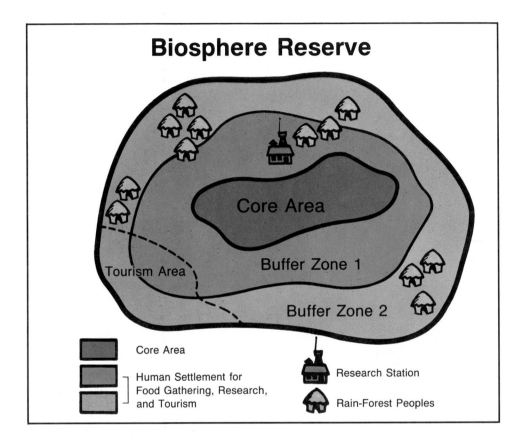

Biosphere Reserve

Core Area

Tourism Area

Buffer Zone 1

Buffer Zone 2

Core Area

Human Settlement for Food Gathering, Research, and Tourism

Research Station

Rain-Forest Peoples

The United Nations, an international agency, came up with the idea of biosphere reserves. In these protected zones, people combine the production of foods and other goods with strict conservation methods. The inner core area is reserved for native plants and animals and cannot be disturbed. Surrounding the core are buffer zones for human use, where tourism, food gathering, and research take place. Biosphere reserves offer a way for people and rain forests to live in harmony with one another.

In general, rain-forest soils are too poor for farming. But in places where forests have been disturbed or destroyed, new types of small-scale planting might allow farmers to support themselves on a single plot. For example, researchers in some sections of Brazil are trying to grow breadfruit or beach palms. These tree crops thrive in poor soils and produce edible fruits. The farming practices of some rain-forest peoples might give further ideas for agricultural experiments.

WE NEED TO KNOW MORE

Saving the rain forests requires that people understand rain-forest communities. Researchers continue to identify rain-forest species and to search for additional uses of rain-forest products. Scientists, for example, are working with local healers to identify plants that may yield new medicines. The healers, who have long collected rain-forest plants to treat illnesses, have a broad knowledge to share with scientists.

Researchers are also finding ways to help rain-forest species survive in preserves. These experts believe preserves that cover less than 60 acres (24 hectares) are too small to permit many animals and plants to reproduce. These smaller preserves may lose up to half of their species within 100 years.

All conservation efforts cost money, and many tropical nations are too poor to fund

An Indonesian healer chips away the bark of a rain-forest tree, which he will eventually make into a medicine.

Important tropical research takes place at a scientific station in Costa Rica's cloud forests.

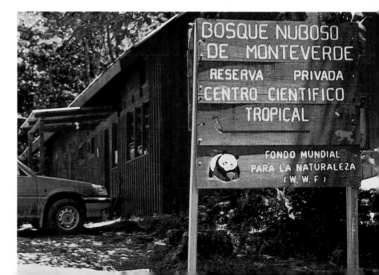

these activities. For this reason, financial help often comes from richer countries. People have raised money for rain-forest conservation in many ways. Some organizations encourage people to "adopt" specific rain-forest acres to protect them. Other groups support agencies in tropical countries that are directly involved in the effort to save the rain forests.

Nature-based tourism has become an additional source of income for countries that are trying to protect their rain forests. People from nations that have no rain forests pay money to visit carefully managed tropical preserves. The money that people spend on their trip shows tropical governments that the forests can be an ongoing source of income in ways that are not harmful.

A **debt-for-nature swap**—exchanging a tropical country's debts for new conservation programs—also funds rain-forest protection. The swap works like this. Many tropical countries have borrowed large sums of money from international banks and then have been unable to repay the

ADOPTING RAIN FORESTS TO SAVE THEM

It may be hard to see what an ordinary person can do to save rain forests. This problem didn't seem to bother Omar Castillo of Mexico, Roland Tiensuu of Sweden, or Jiro Nakayama of Japan. These three students and thousands of others throughout the world participate in programs that allow people to "adopt" acres of Central American rain forest to preserve them.

Here's how the programs work. For a set fee, usually between $30 and $50, a person or group pays for the protection of one acre (about one-half hectare) of rain forest for a year. Some students have recycled cans and newspapers to fund their "adoption." The adoption fee helps a tropical country to hire and train forest rangers and to educate local people about caring for the forest. The money also funds research about how to safely use the rain forests.

The Nature Conservancy runs an adopt-an-acre project and helps to operate the International Children's Rainforest Program. Through these activities, students throughout the world—from New York, New York, to Nagano, Japan—have saved thousands of acres of rain forest in Central America.

debts. The banks are anxious to get back at least part of their money. They agree to erase a portion of the debt for a small amount of cash. A conservation group in a rich country pays the cash. The tropical country then owes its debt to the conservation group, which trades the debt for programs that ensure rain-forest conservation. Debt-for-nature swaps have been successful in Bolivia, Madagascar, and Costa Rica.

Students have used money from recycling aluminum cans to pay for the adoption of rain-forest acres.

CHAPTER SIX

SAVING THE RAIN FORESTS

There are many ways that individuals —alone or as members of concerned groups—can become involved in efforts to save the rain forests. Educate yourself and those around you about the many benefits of healthy, thriving rain forests. This awareness adds to their chances for survival. People can pressure governments and international organizations through letter-writing campaigns, demonstrations, and **boycotts.**

Boycotts occur when large numbers of people stop buying products that harm

(Left) Demonstrations against the abuse of forests have brought this issue worldwide attention. (Right) This young ocelot, a member of an endangered cat species, lives in South America's rain forests. Hunters kill ocelots for their fur. By refusing to buy furs made from ocelots, we participate in efforts to save the animals.

rain forests. For example, Burger King—a major fast-food chain—added beef raised on cleared Central American rain forests to its hamburgers. Some people quit buying Burger King's hamburgers to show their disapproval. Because of the boycott, the company gave up using Central American beef in 1987. Since then, Burger King has worked with Costa Rica's government

People in New York City rally to fight the clearing of rain forests in Brazil.

to find a less-destructive way to provide beef to the U.S. market.

Worldwide public pressure through letters and other activities also influenced the Scott Paper Company, an international paper producer. The firm decided not to participate in an Indonesian industrial project that would have produced wood pulp from as much as a million acres (404,700 hectares) of rain forest.

Before these companies felt public pressure, however, they helped to destroy many thousands of acres of tropical rain forest. Only now, with public awareness and public participation, have these firms changed their policies.

Tropical governments, international banks, and timber-importing firms are also feeling the pressure to halt deforestation. Public campaigns are forcing Japan—the biggest importer of tropical timber—to control its massive logging operations and to stop producing throw-away goods from rain-forest trees. Public demonstrations and letter-writing campaigns pressure international banks—major funders of tropical industrial projects—to rethink their loan policies. Nevertheless, some governments, timber importers, and international banks continue to support projects that destroy rain forests.

WHAT CAN WE DO?

Here are a few suggestions about what all of us can do to preserve our rain forests and to reduce the negative impact we have on our environment. How we live and what we buy make a difference.

JOIN AND SUPPORT CONSERVATION ORGANIZATIONS. Some of these groups work throughout the world to save rain forests. They often have programs that work directly to stop rain-forest destruction.

WRITE LETTERS. Put pressure on influential governments, people, and agencies to stop promoting rain-forest destruction. Tell your governmental representatives to support laws and foreign-aid packages that help tropical countries to preserve their forests. Ask these officials to pressure inter-

Some ice-cream companies have developed new flavors that include rain-forest nuts. These products show that, when protective methods are used, people can make a profit from the forests without harming them.

national banks to fund only those projects that safeguard the natural environment.

BUY PRODUCTS THAT ARE COLLECTED FROM RAIN FORESTS WITHOUT HARMING THEM. The fact that these products, such as beauty aids and food, support preservation of the forests is likely to be marked on the package.

BOYCOTT PRODUCTS THAT DESTROY RAIN FORESTS. For example, many valuable tropical timber species end up as patio furniture. Encourage your parents to avoid buying furniture or tableware made of rain-forest hardwoods, such as teak, rosewood, and mahogany.

REDUCE, REUSE, RECYCLE, DO WITHOUT. People in the United States throw out 432,000 tons (392,000 metric tons) of garbage every day. By using fewer resources, we reduce the need to harvest rain forests and other natural communities.

USE OTHER TRANSPORTATION BESIDES CARS. Exhaust from cars adds CO_2 to our atmosphere, worsening the greenhouse effect. Mass-transit systems—buses, subways, and trains—are good alternatives to cars because they carry many people at once. And bicycles are the cleanest and cheapest form of transportation.

As we clear rain forests, we remove trees that absorb some of the world's CO_2. By planting trees—even if they are not in rain forests—we can help to reduce CO_2 in the atmosphere.

PLANT TREES. Fully grown trees use up some of the CO_2 created by burning coal, petroleum, and rain forests. In addition, trees decrease erosion. They are also natural coolants, because their shade provides a way to keep cool without the use of fans or air conditioners.

ORGANIZATIONS

CONSERVATION INTERNATIONAL
1015 18th Street NW, Suite 1000
Washington, D.C. 20036

THE NATURE CONSERVANCY
1815 North Lynn Street
Arlington, Virginia 22209

CULTURAL SURVIVAL INC.
11 Divinity Avenue
Cambridge, Massachusetts 02138

RAINFOREST ACTION NETWORK
301 Broadway, Suite A
San Francisco, California 94133

ENVIRONMENTAL DEFENSE FUND
257 Park Avenue South
New York, New York 10010

RAINFOREST ALLIANCE
270 Lafayette Street, Suite 512
New York, New York 10012

NATIONAL AUDUBON SOCIETY
950 Third Avenue
New York, New York 10022

**WORLD WILDLIFE FUND/
CONSERVATION FOUNDATION**
1250 24th Street NW
Washington, D.C. 20037

Photo Acknowledgments

Photographs are used courtesy of: p. 4, NASA; p. 6, 8 (left and right), 36, 43 (left and right), 49, Steve Brosnahan; p. 9, 22 (right), 41–42, Edward S. Ross; p. 12 (top), R. Heinrich/FAO; p. 12 (bottom), 16, 55, Pete Carmichael; p. 13 (top), 17, 33, Inter-American Development Bank; p. 13 (middle), Philippine Department of Tourism, Manila; p. 13 (bottom), Jamaica Tourist Board; p. 14, The Digit Foundation; p. 15 (left), Barry Hewlett; p. 15 (right), UNICEF; p. 18, Perry J. Reynolds; p. 19, © 1991 David Julian/Rainforest Alliance; p. 21, 22 (left), James H. Carmichael; p. 23, Dr. Russell A. Mittermeier/Conservation International; p. 24, Richard O. Bierregaard; p. 26 (top), Mike R. Rassier; p. 26 (bottom), Sally Humphrey; p. 27 (top), World Bank; p. 27 (bottom), Ken Meter; p. 28, Ivan Ussach/Rainforest Alliance; p. 29, L. Taylor/FAO; p. 30, 60, American Lutheran Church; p. 32, Hugi Olafsson; p. 34, 51 (right), 62, Leonard Soroka; p. 35, 48, World Wildlife Fund; p. 37, Gail Shumway; p. 38, Miranda Smith Productions, Inc.; p. 39, John Ryle/The Hutchison Library; p. 40, E. Barriga; p. 44, Independent Picture Service; p. 45, Ch. Errath/FAO; p. 46, Frans Lanting-Minden Pictures; p. 51 (left), The Hutchison Library; p. 53, Wisconsin Department of Natural Resources; p. 54, Mark Ludak/Impact Visuals; p. 56, Robert Fox/Impact Visuals; p. 57, Glenn Moody; p. 58, Barry Nehr/USDA Forest Service; p. 61, Ruth Karl. Charts and illustrations: p. 10–11, 20, 31, Laura Westlund; 50, Bryan Liedahl.

Front Cover: Richard O. Bierregaard
Back Cover: (left) L. Taylor/FAO; (right) Gail Shumway

biodiversity (by-o-dih-VER-sih-tee): the condition that occurs when a natural community contains many different kinds of living things.

biosphere reserve: a conservation area that has an inner, reserved zone in the middle and surrounding outer zones, which humans are allowed to use.

boycott: an action by groups or individuals who refuse to buy products from a certain company as a way to express disapproval of the company's policies.

canopy (KAN-uh-pee): the high cover of leafy branches formed by the tops of trees.

Bright orange flames light the evening sky as a rain forest burns in West Africa.

carbon dioxide (CO$_2$): a gas that is naturally found in the air and that also comes from burning trees, from running vehicles on gasoline, and from exhaling.

cloud forest: a forest that is located in mountainous areas of the tropics, where heavy mists occur.

debt-for-nature swap: an arrangement whereby a conservation group pays off part of a tropical country's debt to an international bank, and, in return, the tropical country agrees to fund conservation programs.

deforestation: the large-scale cutting and burning of trees.

dipterocarp (DIP-teh-row-karp): a tall tree of Southeast Asia that yields timber, oils, and other products.

endemic species: a plant or animal that survives and breeds only in a small, specific area or in a rare habitat.

epiphyte (EP-ih-fite): a plant that grows on another plant but that gets its food from the air.

erosion (ih-RO-zhun): the wearing away or washing away of soil by water or wind.

Ants have established a tall hill as their habitat in the forests of Nigeria, West Africa.

extinct: no longer existing.

extractive reserve: a protected piece of land from which workers can harvest products under careful management.

greenhouse effect: the result of the sun's heat becoming trapped in the earth's atmosphere by gases in the same way that glass traps heat in a greenhouse.

habitat: a natural setting that provides the necessities of life for plants and animals.

hydroelectric dam: a barrier across a river that converts the power of flowing water into electrical energy.

jungle: forested land with dense vegetation near the forest floor.

latex: a milky, white substance that comes from several types of tropical trees and that can be made into products such as rubber or chewing gum.

liana (lee-AHN-uh): a climbing plant that twists itself around the trunk of a rain-forest tree.

lymphocytic leukemia (lim-fo-SIT-ik loo-KEE-mee-uh): a form of cancer in which certain white blood cells grow in an uncontrolled way and badly affect the behavior of other blood cells in the human body.

logging: large-scale cutting of trees for lumber.

lowland evergreen forest: a forest in the tropics that has high rainfall levels throughout the year.

nature-based tourism: a money-earning program that arranges carefully managed visits to fragile natural communities, such as rain forests.

nutrient: a substance used as food by plants and animals.

pesticide (PES-ti-side): a chemical used to destroy insects or other pests.

photosynthesis (fote-o-SIN-thuh-suss): the chemical process by which green plants make their own food. The process involves the reaction of CO_2, water, and sunlight.

primate: a member of a mammal group that includes humans, apes, and lemurs.

resettlement: the process of moving people to a new place.

seasonal rain forest: a forest in the tropics with a definite, annual dry period that slows plant growth.

slash-and-burn farming: an agricultural plan in which farmers clear, burn, and plow land before planting crops. The crops survive for only a few seasons, and the land is then abandoned for a new acreage.

species (SPEE-sheez): a kind of living thing.

sustainable development: the use of a resource, such as a tropical rain forest, so that it can produce goods continuously without hurting the balance of nature.

topsoil: the surface layer of dirt in which plants grow.

tropical rain forest: a dense woodland with high amounts of annual rainfall—at least 80 inches (203 centimeters), but often much more. These forests contain tall evergreen trees and many other plants and a wide variety of animals.

tropics: the hot, wet region that forms a belt around the earth's equator.

A fallen tree from a tropical rain forest in South America shows its short buttress roots.

INDEX